Sweetgum & Lightning

Sweetgum & Lightning

Rodney Terich Leonard

Four Way Books
Tribeca

Library of Congress Cataloging-in-Publication Data

Names: Leonard, Rodney Terich, author.
Title: Sweetgum & lightning / Rodney Terich Leonard.
Other titles: Sweetgum and lightning
Description: [New York] : [Four Way Books], [2021] |
Identifiers: LCCN 2020037842 | ISBN 9781945588747 (trade paperback)
Subjects: LCGFT: Poetry.
Classification: LCC PS3612.E5744 S94 2021 | DDC 811/.6--dc23
LC record available at https://lccn.loc.gov/2020037842

This book is manufactured in the United States of America and printed on
acid-free paper.

"Kiss Me To The Music" by George Henry Jackson, Earl Forest, and
Richard Smythe Kuebler
Copyright © 1989 by Malaco Music, Inc. and Peermusic III, Ltd.
Peermusic III, Ltd. administers on behalf of itself and Malaco Music, Inc.
Used by Permission. All Rights Reserved.

Four Way Books is a not-for-profit literary press. We are grateful for the assistance
we receive from individual donors, public arts agencies, and private foundations.

This publication is made possible with public funds from the
National Endowment for the Arts

and from the New York State Council on the Arts, a state agency,

We are a proud member of the Community of Literary Magazines and Presses.

Contents

To Ruby Edwards Leonard
for supporting my life & spirit

It's almost too much,
too much to believe.

—Bobby "Blue" Bland
"Kiss Me to the Music"

Language beside the language

In da first place—
I come from baghetti & banounce
baze & baff whutta
from chullen, pitiation & clare fo god
from coosa county yall, dem & nem
dem mine—aint—big mama nem
from stankin & breff, lil bit mo
from saushit, winnies, avoid da popo
from deddy, aynee, dat dare & frune
who got da body—what time da frune iah?
from valemtines, feets, taters & okree
from coveralls & my stomach toe up
from yonda, good moanya, spensis things
from draws & how come ms roof so observative?
from sastificate, soditty, reefah & daplooma
from skrange, prestripshun, skrawberry bloomahs
from done fell out at da hosspill
better gwone now & eat dem grits
from dis here my house
git yo fangah outta my face
from got my check they cut me real bad
from foaf Sunday meetin
from "preciation outta be give when da church is full"

Norphenia's Lament

i.

Oh, to plate potatoes & pot roast
for a trunk-armed man of pine—
pecs & dangle
seek dawn & terrain;
the planet they find is pecan
underneath orange & aqua cotton.
Winter nightgown draws the heat.

ii.

Quick-turn—
Norphenia in a mudhole spinning.
Wheeze & Black decaf.

Three-year air & slack
in the seat of culottes:
What can the matter be, now?

It can't be too serious
We can't talk it over.
Now is now-scented swoon.

iii.

—1969—
September-sealed envelope
postmarked El Paso, Fort Bliss.
Really—
a letter & a lil' piece of change
should nurse a vow,
hush a woman's worry?
Whyless husband meant
rented rooms, in laws sofa
Buick burdened with bedspreads
bomber jackets, kimonos
teapots & pictures—
wife-wait,
stoops roost.

iv.

Rundown Mama—
third shift
ten to six at the Russell Mills.
Glistened & glistening press & curl.
Whiffs of frangipani.

Pork rinds & Schlitz.
Many a day chime & reachable chapel;
six sisters are not scars nor welts.
For wishes she won't possess,
Otis Redding cups vinegar into Friday,
the day Sunday through Thursday makes.

      v.

Separation

      separates.

Legs
weren't always crossed.

Note from Norphenia: *Everything's Out in the Open*

Early wiggle of light
more silver than clabbered dreams.

New suits, cowboy boots and Polaroid
sent you packing your hair with Vaseline.

Notches up on mother wit and born fourth.
Between us the pull of secrecy:

hands with which I played adult;
the other day man with thick thumbs—

those of *your* father.
I watched you teach and paddle trees

polished your crown of tantrums with spoil:
another tape recorder, another mitt

another book this November.
Motherhood's tacit scratch.

Lunch Menu: Summer 1977

Spam
ribbon cane
popcorn & hot sauce
cucumbers & dill pickles
side-of-the-road picked plums
knife-sliced fried potatoes
boiled peanuts
mayonnaise & ketchup sandwiches
white rice w/salt, pepper & butter
Vienna Sausage & Saltine crackers
frozen sugar-sweetened white milk
baked store-stolen yams

Pie & Pap Marbury's Daughter

Calliphoridae—blow flies
buzz the smokehouse
for bacon, breast & neck
for dead oink & cluck.

Lightning belongs to Jesus
'round here.
Pie's zucchini is squash.
Pap's venison is deer.

Pregnant Barbara
sheens gullible flanking
patience & bloom,
coquettish as a hatched hen egg.

Swirl of sea salt under her tongue,
power saw oil, lard, onion-fried pink salmon,
the smell of morning chicken shit yanks her vomit.
Not soothed by chancel nor bagpipes

If it ain't rural it ain't right.
Hand to hold on simple Sundays,

She
is Pie & Pap Marbury's daughter.

Hula Hoop Children

Thumb suckers & inside pant players
spin through the air on merry-go-rounds—
nip their affection
for after-school television
as if anesthetized by cotton candy.

You know them; they chew boogers.

*

Boy-to-boy pajama dreams
they come here switching
khaki gestures
of someone else's embarrassment.
One Thanksgiving, in 1978, I asked if I could marry a cousin.

Asked in the company of dentures & frowns
amid mounds of meats & starches & sweets
hell broke loose
in a roomful of *what-the-f's*
potato salad on lapels & the floor
onions & gravy gone to waste!

This is not good
I say.

*

Who are these limber children
mouthing for meat
in mash season
whose spasms for drama are tulips & precise?

Hula Hoop Children—
argyle & polyester, platforms & rouge
some Saturday
they'll
twist & purple their locs.

Pink Chenille

She of Ecclesiastes & cream-colored envelope,
the mother mails
to summer cousin—
cash, food stamps, regards:

    Dear Shirley,
Your bosom is
a great big city, pink chenille
for other folks' children. Six weeks of pillowed
nights to dream of freeways, malts & shortstop,
my son jumped off the sighing Greyhound belching Sunkist,
Patrina & Pea-Eye, his new bus-seat friends—
belief & noise stuck to his chest, yelling he'd thumbed
way back to basement-paneled Sixteenth Street Baptist:
Cynthia, Carol & Carole & Addie Mae—back to 15 September 1963.

    Child, came home chirping Five Points South,
UAB, Thirteenth Avenue North, Dynamite Hill,
Legion Field & Dr. A.G. Gaston:
Part of all you earn is yours to keep.
The truth is red:
Next to *them that's got shall get*, I twitch.

You wear raven silk taut at the nape of the neck.

In wards of Pac-Man, Adidas, & Atari,
you ushered in this rattle of awe—
glorious Black Fever!
     Glorious—

        Yours,

XI

An outhouse year.
Someone I love rips rags for tampons.
Someone I love speaks less & less.

Is the sky
ever too pink
to suggest you're poor?

I am eleven—
having studied them
I introduce myself to Colonel Douglas R. and Jessica K. Smith
husband & wife
of Rockfords Golden Rule Market—
the Smiths of Asprey & Chanel
cashmere & city speech
of Beethoven's italicized wonderment
I know because I asked
of Black-chauffeured blue Cadillac
& 2 Doberman Pinschers
guarding their brick Federal Colonial.

I am hired.
To neaten & clean,

to stock & cashier—
sometimes I pump gas.

On calendar-circled Saturdays
I utter Eames, rattan, Picasso
bone china, commissary, sparkle, miso
lacquer, Andrew Wyeth, linseed oil
poached, Shakespeare, Melba toast
duvet, Summer's Eve, Harper Lee
salmon, invoice, Unleaded, Visa.

Slowly
I inch
my family away
        from
government
milk & cheese.

Manners Tilt Country

In this house manners tilt country:
fig preserves faint on biscuits,
stop looking down my throat,
a child's chair clear of grown-talk.

The patterns of two left feet,
six & seven-year hands,
cousins in the settled dust.
Black ants circle American

sweetgum & lightning,
plural of tock, loses
its temper & gongs
the jug's metal dipper.

Grandma Viska—
Emma, Mattie, & Queen Esther's mother,
frocks pink & black bonnets,
pulls heat & poison from wounds.

Wonder why
she morning-rakes

the front yard
with cloth-tied brush brooms?

Viska Martin Edwards
1889-1978

Hummer of Anyone Decisive: 1915-1990

My grandfather—
John Walter Edwards strummed the guitar
under a sycamore tree.
City trash-truck worker,
curer of thrushes' problems,
brought directly to holder & folder of his wallet,
my grandmother, Mary Emma.

New to the rise of millennium-ripped questions,
memory is technological; it lurks & it forgives
dilution & tint—
I have some questions from all the grandchildren:
Were you atheist or agnostic?
In your sphere, God was nowhere?
Why the austerity, so few words?

Leo-born to tempt & deter—
        John to wife,
Daddy to Catherine
Willie Doris, Ruby
Johnnie Mae & Mary
Elizabeth, Dezzie & Louise.
        Mr. John
to weekend women

& back porch bathers—
lithe hummer
of anyone decisive,
you sucked raw eggs.

Intro to empty:
your mother's portrait, above
a bed, straight-nailed to the wall,
& never a ringing rotary—
did *without*,
as a way of being,
heal anything?

Young sergeant of Grand Forks,
here the tall tan men are sun
& though private, I am no secret.
          "Big Deddy,"
this legacy of amours & faulting
darts my tumult.

The Late Mrs. Clarence Jackson, Sr. Speaks to Her Grandson in a Dream on a Ferry from Dover to Calais

The mannish way
my son phoned you
quiet legs crossed
funk in his drawers
six o'clock news on
pulls up my onions.

Each time I spit & cuss
each pour of Clorox
each Meals on Wheels
each quip of my name
—Willow Mae—
is hallowed gossip.

Weeks I smelled glory:
ham hocks & souse
honey buns & fatback
chitlins & hushpuppies
Pepsi & fried chops—
loves I lost my legs to.

Fastened to Roots, Love & Story:
Mother Recalls a Ten-Pound Storm

Midwife of scarce warmth,
Mrs. Wilson's lamplight air.
Her cod-liver tongue, talcum bosom
& cursive note of thorny expectations:
Come see me when I can best assist.
Bring two, bleached sheets.
My fee in 1970 a hundred dollars.

Aretha's "I Say a Little Prayer"
Salt & sautée my mother's lilt.
Closer to thirty than strength,
I straddle a stool; Salem's ashes
Flicked in hair-grease top
Fastened to roots, love & story.
It's Thursday before Thanksgiving—

Each half-mile, (she walks to & fro),
The moon, a vat of pelvic threat.
Scheduled curls oil the world.
Baby between thumb & formula,
The same day catching her & stove
Singing mismatched ditties: Yams
Meatloaf. *Before I put on my makeup*
The moment I wake up.

Domesticoustics

a. (1997)

Arrival at twenty-one
cocks his tam sideways.
Deep-freeze nod
to alley deacons & white folks.
Terry Derell
strums corduroy-gray
acoustics.
Chlora is his tiramisu—
he's indiscriminate
pot & vodka-cranberry wise.

b. (2012)

Maria Inés
backhanded the hurt—
hyena-laughing.
Common shoulders
glittered for night-prerequisites.
Eye sockets
house sass-glass.
Her Louboutin's are hers.
Jazz is novel nectar.
Moon-swayed—she's absosucculent.

c. (1974)

Snatched from
tight-eyed scribble,
water boils,
china shards scrape,
white kittens meow.
What night is this, Rodney?
Amid jumbo pencils,
red satchel & Crayola,
candy corn & wide-lined,
pee-wet paper,
my mama's teeth
sweep the linoleum.

Lord, Have Mercy: Don't Go to Hell Cramped Up

Father, 1959

Daddy loads, cocks, & aims his gun.
Four young girls & their baby brother
trace the woods
by mercy of the moon.

Briar-torn legs bleed a simpler truth:
no enjoying June today.
Ever smiled an alcoholic into
burying his flask & bully?
Probably easier to patty-cake with the sun.

Son, 1999

He tongues the last cubes
of Johnny Walker's twist & trick.
Sleep rinses his eyes yellow-pain clear.
Own pail to pull,
bobby pin headed toward the eardrum,
the clack of dominoes,
bones on the table.

The twenty-year deal:
sober hell & jail at fifty—
alphabets to learn, *son* uttered strangely,
swallowed whole.
                    Ghosts
to shotgun
again.

Bumble o' Names

a seven-beat song

Bobo, Meat, Potato-Chip
Tootle, Choo, Pee Wee, Throaty
Nessa, Lumpty, Grease, Big-Man
Tuneya, Fattie, Bucky, Pie
Grit, Frog, Tit, Good Gooch, LaJit,
Spam, Bo, Red, Mighty-Mixer
Shell, C-C, Noodah, Knock-Knee
Weedy, Junebug, Lee Pap, Grip
Roll 'em, Big-Boy, Poonie-Eyes
Boonty, Sistah, Beebo, Scoop
Dunchy, Bappy, Britches, Poot
Barefeet, Creesie, Tatty, Pig
            singin
Sugar-Man, San-Nan, Popeye
Pokie, Scooter, Missy, Rell
Reesie, Haircut, Uptown, Hess
Baldy, Bad-Shape, Mr. Square
Sweetie, Shawty, Badfoot, Oont
Boochie, Bear-Mouth, Doll-Baby
Punkin, Pilly, Pudd'n, Kway
Redhead, Lay-Low, Mall, He-Stank
Bow-Leg, Bay-Boy, Dibba, Twelve
Meat-Skins, Fast-Ass, Dank, Low-Nuts
Lightnin', TuShake, Bare-Mouth, Mimp
Pookie, DuShake, Milk-Leg, Simp.

After Ben Webster's 1959
Rendition of "Time After Time"

      Back to sisters, brothers, & cousins
riding the rear seat of a shiny green
"fly-me-baby"—Alabama for Cadillac—
I get it—
I tell myself that I'm so lucky.
The yesterglance details cool well water,
tadpoles dandy & dancing between my fingers.

      I wear a 1975 Fourth of July outfit:
red shorts short
an old 69¢ tank top
blue red & yellow flip flops,
headed for a dirt baseball field,
waiting for fried fish
with hot grease, hot sauce
& French's mustard,
clutching white bread,
25¢ Chek cream soda
iced in tubs to freeze the head.

      I crave banana pudding,
The Three Little Pigs,

cleats,
& the finger-grip of ten-speed jokes,
cracked in the *ah-ha* of kid silly.

    I rememorize
Armour Funeral Home's phone number—
recite, by heart, their church-fan motto:
Where the warmth, beauty
spaciousness & the convenience
of our facilities cost no more.

    Miss Mae Sal & Ida Bell,
voodoo women mixing
cat's blood & hair grease
menses & collard greens
folks neighing like horses
ceilings painted haint blue.

    Shirtless football,
mowed lawns for trips to Six Flags,
pass-me-down Lee's starched heavy;
William & Jimmy

Berdrell & James
brothers rushed in their hearses.
Aunt Catherine's mile-wide holler.

    Way back goes back to William Bell:
I've got a woman at home sweet as can be
a woman on the outside crazy about me.
Momma knew why Daddy sang that song;
one & one & one equals zero.

    August is an eighth girdle for Grandma,
280 & too pearish for gabardine.
New Style Baptist Church,
head-to-toe revival-blue,
God phloxed her plea & tremble:
Come what may,
shepherd us shank & mountain,
in wee & tall steps,
ever mindful.

    I've not been lost to skyscrapers
or continents,
under no need to forgive the soil of Coosa,
dry cough between us.

Language—
the pep I've craved most,
its kindred cheer unheard.
Silence's consequence—
we slip from relevance.

Tanqueray #3

Sober for most of the day,
I've got that left-eye look again.
Am told I've turned mercurial.
My father & I are textured landscapes,
who we are *not* to each other, keloid-like.
At twenty, he helped to make my broad shoulders.

Forgiveness, hill that it is, no longer needles.
The climb between us isn't the hard part;
memory catalogues first-hurts in decibels—
all those untrained Sunday Sopranos,
kinfolk & not
warned
that a shut-door in the country
can't fasten secrets.

Mom gets pregnant at a Birmingham motel,
her separated husband
somewhere
unzipping some other
Mattie's bra.

The nerve & detail of what we remember—

& with this Thursday
comes a ritual,
Tanqueray #3:
slant claims my neck
I lose my manners
& re-pop this blister
about dad & lil' LaWanna,
some un-talked-about shit
still curdled in my craw.

Last time we spoke in 1996,
the day I got some bad news
over a glass of scotch & milk
he mumbled something about
how my ways
water-down his last name.

Black men
& surnames—
you can't buy back
a pawned sunset.

I left the midwife's
with another man's

last name
      & by now
I'm crunk—
it's my birthday.

The past
creeps wild
in my eyes.

To a Cousin on His Forty-Sixth

Deuteronomy, inner-dream hypnotist,
is apathy for the less fortunate.
Homeboys make do with leaky suitcases
dapping through mud & water
hollers & pews to the haze of March
Times Square Room 718,
reaching for anise-julep, Saturday-Sunday.

I find your wide hands coarse, gentle soldiers.
They have gutted hogs, split oaks,
baked cakes, pitched baseballs, break
danced, dribbled & barbered,
caressed your wife, cultivated two sons.
What won't last always—
do you believe trauma

trickles down generationally?
The roots & wings of my life clenched
between anathema & superstition—
chaos erupts where salt is spilled.
Running from bait & tackle, I wrote a poem.
Did your father ever cry?
What color were his eyes?

Privy to septuagenarian banter,
seems like you radioed ahead,
clear that static is static.
After Pokey Bear's "My Sidepiece,"
a bone for the folks back home—
pick up where you left off
on Playa del Amor in Cabo.

Express Yourself
Express Yourself

—Charles Wright & The Watts 103rd Street Rhythm Band, 1970

Hot Metal Cools Slowly into Law

                        Neither gin
nor its companion elixirs—tonic, rickey, juice, fizz,
soothes like warm air parting the hair,
primping the fades of soldiers stationed
stateside or overseas.

                    Content & wary of rank & reveille
mess halls, protocol, & lust,
alongside efforts of spit shine & conformity,
our natural needs are natural,
sir yes sir   yes sir yes   reports-as-ordered sir.

                    For matters of trick, shade, & shadow—
wink & nod, spread the hiss
down-low
palm-scratch
shoosh
find-a-match
shoosh
tilt the blue beret that-a-way.

                    Sing-sing-sing of erasure's thirst—
Keg of August wind, heat in his hips, for once,
a dog-days storm. *Muddy water in my shoes, but see,*

it's baptismal to requite someone's swinging-sweep,
another fella's good "get-down."

       Sing-sing-sing of a time in Roswell, TDY—
He was a major who read Capote & called him Streckfus.
Next to my arm lay his on which prodigious Kansas grew.
Where there is no shame scandal tames its wince.
At parade rest, left foot to the left of the right foot,
I fed my ego a trip to our haunt, the far-end silverleaf oak,
its bark beckoning for both of our backs,
lunar taboo—officer & enlisted waltzing in the lion's den:
If morning's echo says we've sinned,
just touch my cheek before you leave me.

       We also candle & pant in his tent—
       And it won't matter anyhow—

The translatable hush of Clinton's decree:
"Effective immediately,
brave men & women, defenders in peace & war,
fully serve this country stanchioning off your nature
& essence, these fundamental urges & gasps.
Choose your trot, mild, spicy, or hot.
Fuck whomever you choose—
Don't Ask Don't Tell. "

39

Response to Miss Eady's Every-Sunday Question, "How are you?"

Fifth rum & slow piano
shoo haints outta my head.
Ever felt the curt masculinity
of hurt latched onto your navel?

You must be scorched hearing
when times were toothsome
as wild salmon & couscous,
about a lone leaf skating Amsterdam's

Canals, the small hand of the clock,
7 pm, each July, tucking under collars
at the North Sea Jazz Festival.
About lavender & peppermint tub soaks,

& the auburn-creased refrigerator note:
We are us whether loved or lonely.
I was always a veteran worrier,
wide within winter waters, Miss Eady,

nibbling & gnawing on memory:
Apartment 5-C on 73rd & 5th
whistled mattress & magnum
tuition & food again.

Elegy for Sabena

1969-2007

> *eyes, loud-soft, with crying and with smiles.*
> —Gwendolyn Brooks

Sixty-months of a dreamed glare,
    away from Manhattan and Columbus,
        avenues slick with year-round verse,
            way up in back of the Poconos.

Much on which to muse,
    much for the notebook,
        always some other someone,
            wasn't always easy.

January was picturesque:
    squirrels threw bark into snow-covered brooks,
        cooing daughter, clapping son,
            Benjamin & Nina tickled toward warm-day stitches.

Away from Manhattan and Columbus,
    amid kitchen-counter TV,
        at the tail end of "Happy Birthday,"
            each absence swollen.

Military Sexual Trauma:
(MST) Per the Department of Veterans Affairs

Three airmen styrofoaming cheap BX wine,
How did sip come into that night?
How come moon how come me?
Sliding into a hill I was sliding.
The last light I shoved
Boots laced for ceremony
Varnished for inspection
Templed toward two hills
The girths of West Virginia
Bearded & mustached—
And him & him were white.

How. Did sip. Come into that night—
A sly pill against your will is a lowdown thing.
Desert Storm's hoodooed pour.
Runny insomnia. What wasn't red?
Red was viscous
And crimson & crawling everywhere.
Where are my dog tags?
It was August of 1991.
My notebook was black.
Called the First Sergeant.
Major Opalenik was mandatory.

Wartime staffing was critical.
And there was Chaplain Prez.
And Chaplain Prez prattled
Let's live through this, young man.
And I rearranged my room.
And my next notebook was black.
And I boomboxed Nina Simone.
And earned my marksmanship ribbon.
And my rifle dreams saw faces:
The two bastards from West Virginia.
And no man was safe with me.

Bird Alone

With no mate
Turning corners tempting fate
Flying circles in the air
Are you on your way somewhere?
—Abbey Lincoln

New to the ambience of live jazz,
I twitch as Abbey in all-black
stylizes her *no mate*. My sweater's neck
is thrift-picked, sink-wet.

Purring these *corners* & *circles*,
& by the time she glides *somewhere*,
I've suppressed enough winter mucus
to engine a pop & ugly-cry.

Miss Lincoln's trio:
Marc Cary on piano
Michael Bowie on bass
Jaz Sawyer on drums.

Oud uncorked '99.
In this place darkness is coy

with its shape & shadow;
the unuttered is fodder for clef.

My gray-banged,
Blue Note tablemate
taps my right leg, leans in, whispers
Hold on, man, she's just getting started.

Day Dream

Deep in a rosy glow
          —Duke Ellington

I had this same daydream last year—
whether we should go ahead and once this fire.
We men are fast gum chewers when with ourselves,
our tones notched down, and what we mute outright

we specify via text or a thumb on the shoulder, rotating.
The gallop from elusive neighbor to slow need
must've started with a tight, beige tunic,
the shorn facial and Caesar.

And the day's newness to two things—
Roach's *Freedom Now Suite* and Twenty-one;
easy to see why hippie parents skip baby talk.
Surely, I had this same daydream last August:

his young woman in Paris and me with me,
whether we should go ahead and once this fire,
fever this urge with a splash of vetiver.
Here, again: we specify and pivot.

The gallop must've nudged Wednesday's randy.
Must've started with Abbey Lincoln's vinyl holler.

2 June 2001: Before *What Happened, Miss Simone?*

Too big a cat to be called a kitten,
nowadays hiring help to dial up
quirks & commands—interviews,
cancelled concerts, defunct royalties,
noise complaints, restraining orders,
pool maintenance, lab results—
in English, in Carry-le-Rouet.

        Introducing
Eunice Kathleen Waymon,
gowning the pains of others,
"Don't You Pay Them No Mind,"
"Mississippi Goddam,"
another champagne flute hurled
& shattered; doll, years beyond hyacinth,
I know you know,
this is not a muscadine city,
everybody don't love you,
"Young, Gifted and Black"
& "Jim Crow" are on iTunes,
pardon my tone—
You don't wanna meet your papa drunk.

2 pm
57 East 57 th Street

I bet you a sumo wrestler's siesta,
someone got her *second-order* right:
Armand de Brignac Blanc de Blancs,
de-stemmed strawberries,
honey dew,
kale & mustard greens,
champignon soup,
basmati rice.
Vertamae Grosvenor's fried chicken.

Suite Talk—
I'm ready, light my cigarette.
Cayenne & honey in the Darjeeling, please.

They told Bobby Womack he wasn't
'commercial, commercial, commercial,
no you're not commercial.'

My set-lists are mine & not set—
to hell with commercial.

Is Billy Preston still alive
& playing the piano, Clifton?
Draw the curtains, I must rest before the applause.

8 pm

Hep to chafe,
I scan my wonder,
apneic as steamed mascara;
row-to-row spaghetti straps

jeans & suspenders prevail.
I wear black linen.
This day in 1989,
I graduated high school.

Gussied in silver & lilac,
  Miss Simone
greases the Steinway;
Carnegie Hall is hushed to sniff volume.

As for edge—
a horsetail fly whisk from Benin,
not without Langston, Lorraine,

& "I Want a Little Sugar in My Bowl."

Under a cayenne spell,
prim pianistry & rough-wail
blade & bandage,
sleepless & scattered as incense.

Feet betray bunions
pumps & timbs,
wide pleas for *The Desperate Ones*.
The moon belches for two encores

Septembers Ago: America Behaving

for Miss Leontyne Price

Nineteen days after 9/11,
ulcers order and eat their breakfast.
After rain and shards and hearses
bossing the avenues—
we wear perse, dark grayish blue.
Michter's Rye and Nova Scotia Halibut
are 86'ed at Le Bernardin.
Gluttony nipped and deboned,
where can I go without me
is next-week's question?

Dr. Spivey and I aren't finished yet.
I taxi home to a block that's nutmeg raw,
West 132nd Street,
to catch televised and creased confusion–
Giuliani's lisp.
To ink or not the thumbs with pomegranate seeds
while Brokaw and Albright quick-blink and quiver
American Airlines Flight 11~ United Airlines Flight 175
American Airlines 77~ United Airlines 93~ Al-Qaeda~
Pentagon~ Shanksville~ Taliban~ War~ The Towers.

La-la-la-la-la
as opposed to night—
We need somebody to sing us, at least, a song.
Phones the woman of throat from Laurel, Mississippi,
Mary Violet Leontyne Price,
daughter of James Anthony and Katie Baker Price.
A diva gladly trapped in the butter of *Il Trovatore's* Leonora,
Margaret Bonds' "This Little Light of Mine,"
Puccini's "Vissi d'arte" and Samuel Barber's "Despite and Still."
"Good ole Juilliard," she once said.

Weaned from windowsill sunlight,
wherever it is, Sunday fevers for perspective—
this Manhattan day is no different.
Stage curtain drawn Septembers ago,
current of posture and gown
and pearls and orchestra,
present as seventy-four clasped Aida's—
We needed her to sing us, at least, one song.
"I was sensitive enough to leave my era and not have it leave me."
Miss Price *is* "God Bless America" behaving.

Without You, Very Well

after Hoagy Carmichael

It took seven Decembers
three moves
two years of underwear inspection

the Easter sermon on addiction & fear
a sexless Tulum jaunt
the birthday trip to Boston

no synergy, a bruised index finger
and the finality of a Cloisters May bell
to find words for wants that failed us.

Cedarwood & Taurean Cuss

After *Dexter* and YouPorn,
like a spry rabbit in a lettuce
patch—there it stares
this strand of gray
silken & moody
in the lush night-night.
The gall of it flares fret & nostril.

Next to salted beard & mustache,
I hurl Taurean cuss.
Sidled this close to 47,

I've not panted for distinction.

I'd rather Lime-A-Rita than Cuervo.
Indulge NBA only for the high asses.
Elizabeth Alexander sends handwritten thanks.
My Canon pouts for Palermo.

And I have a remedy for a West Coast redeye:
Sachal Vasandani's "Here Comes the Honeyman"
Cinnamon Tea
White Henny
And this decisive text:

home from seattle!
famished
a week without THE pudding!
rain & ash for days
i'm hungry and craving sap

*

—Do stranger's play in your sacred bush?

Intergenerational bewitch;
through fuzz, shag-shadow & kink,
wordless we be
men in the family
sprinkle cedarwood down here.

Carnal in a Time of PrEP

#

M4M—
lights low on my knees or ass up
vgl/ddf   white, 29, gym body
sane & safe ub2   HIV-negative
as of yesterday 10/08/15
love to down & mount BBC
total anonymous here
prefer DL daddy types
cock pic gets reply

#

October's beyond
didanosine
videx ®
stavudine
zerit ®
zidovidine
retrovir ®
we arrive at
tenofovir/emtricitabine

truvada ®
i'm on PrEP

     #

Silver Schwinn leaning against the wall
heels & cheeks glad on a stool
i pipe
we don't kiss
i bite neck
i think i hear
more afraid of desire than dying
i up my grunt
the buzzer read *Canup*
never saw his face

Complexion

Because I don't tissue-paper blame
which gets the drift that no one, alive or
dead, gives a damn, not in my burgundy
suite, where Lit thought he farted but he

shit. The grey in my beard grows here,
is not cosmetic. Someone's daughter moues
on cue but can't return a hug—oh, oh, oh
oh-well, she's not to blame for Lenny's

thong fetish or Camden-born Prince Albert
This poem yachts & swings/dig it, tock it,
pop it taut-and-sagacious, ta git my gravy
I just wanna be jumpseat & aero in my own

historical zoom. Keep your Tonka, Tootsie Roll
& black bandana for the next cowboy—
I bought me a pair of camel suede YSL Jonny
Boots, boo, so stop by my place first, cause

I wanna ski wit you—wary of sirens & shade,
wary of jubilee & leakage, wary of whose-turn,
wary of skeleton keys & Apt. 33-B & Ambien,
wary of white, wary of delusion & corners,

wary of tarot & myrrh, towers & hallelujah,
wary of PTSD—dem bats, cobwebs & cryin
tweakin me—dat Portuguese-Dutch wee-slant
of light in da cells of Elmina Dungeon whirrin me—

b/p: 220/112

She caint pray fa me dat squat nun
grinnin & guttin dat goat;
call da ambalance & right-revn,
read me Ezekiel 16:6:

And when I passed by thee, and saw thee
polluted in thine own blood,
I said unto thee
when thou wast in thy blood, Live.

Heave

Sister—

Since you declined phone calls
flowers & Delta Sigma Theta
tears—
how free & unblocked are you
now that your mama is dead?

Wind-blown Plums

1.

Half-moon—
what's real,
what's right?
I can't clearly
see myself;
memory fails
to fail.

Patrilineal rot—
exhaust-pipe blister,
anti-aloe;
its slurp, whisk, & brawl,
needs kneading from the root.

Underneath the wealth of death,
knuckling his private sadness,
such an indistinguishable snore,
I might pen a Son House remix,
& call it
Clarence Station Jackson, Jr.

That's kelp, has bite.

2.

Mind the month of February,
its hawk, the frigid curvature
of a coroner's baton—

I'll tell you another thing,
young man, seems to me,
your daddy'd been up
in that apartment
more'n a minute, cause
yesterday was President's Day.
Supposedly, somebody seen him

late Saturday night, before sunrise,
Sunday, actually—
Mr. Jackson was with himself
in that apartment,
with the heat on, at least
26-27 hours—
You are the next of kin, yeah?

What you thinking,
a funeral, urn, or graveside?
Be best to proceed with things
with haste.
He's in bad shape—
looks like he left here startled,
with something on his mind.

3.

Gloved hands pat my shoulders—

lifting into view
charms & faults:

another adult prayer & day
at which I wink & mouth,

to the little boy in me, choose
your own scissors & construction paper.

Give Aunt Elizabeth eyes & hair.
Draw smiley faces on bicentennial saucers,

silver stars on sheet-covered end tables.
Will I forever fidget & run away in real time?

4.

Silhouettes of five
Dillard's-bought,
pillbox hats,
erect in stretch-plush,
the family car.
Daughters,
benders of habit.

Second car,
bright headlights.
Grandchildren, in age order,
laurel on each other's
shoulders,
like windblown plums.
Unusual space for an uncle, an only son.

The route from the city
to Elam Baptist
cooped & mesquite,

damp as disobedience.
The ride itself,
charred mulct;
theatre.

From front-seat right,
finger-wave upstage:
They need us to be sturdy.
They, I heat?
The pronoun dumps the bucket,
unfurls my handkerchief;
there is no ecstasy in gasp.

The halt of tires on gravel
cracks open this
rare hour,
when grief's claw
dictates for this family,
departure from wrangle,
a hurricane sorry until.

My Father Liked Me & Loved My Mother: The Last Tension & Say-so with Scent

Goodwater, Alabama.
Riotous vomit & bile.

Things I take—

Two unlabeled VHS tapes
Brownish polyester shirt
Tobacco-filled pipe
Photo albums
Box of papers
Eight Viagras
The knife
The tooth.

"Tooth #18
2nd molar
Lower left quadrant
Extracted with pocketknife.
Sepsis."

My mother takes—

Pots & pans
Laundry detergent

A metallic locket
Fahrenheit cologne
Ralph Lauren pillowcases
Everything electrical,
Rechargeable.

This way Willoughby, Willoughby,
Willoughby,
This way Willoughby,
All night long.

—a children's line song/game

Kamasi, Muscadet, & Mary Lou Williams

In my head rain really lopes & rains
        triangular;
cavity-sensitive but not quite oversexed
        I prefer
clean & singularly-crooked teeth.
        Rarely
does the Old Bay of flesh subdue
        wag & drool.
Grown & habitual—
        I loaf
my bark to consummation & lonely
        riffs lonely.

Long legs agape in a Black man's home—
        the third date—
We have six-more minutes of
        "Leroy and Lanisha,"
Kamasi Washington's brewed-astral bronze.
        Plucky & white of him
to ask no questions, though fits of wow!
        Not the alcoholic
he surmised, my keen interior notions—
        framed black & whites of Blacks,

stacked Kente, nickel-stoked Skylar bar cart
       & ruminations:

The utterance of faggot
       baffles me
keeps Christians in church
       in barriers
of the mind lowers expectations;
       that Jesus can fix it,
glad-Jesus on the cross.
       Is interracial romance
sensible when whom we're able
       to become
is eclipsed by the history
       of whom we are?

     *

He sat upright & semi-tranquil
       through Kamasi
two rounds of Muscadet
       & Mary Lou Williams.
& on the edge of 1930's iron,
       my world

away from the world,
        my bed—
He said:
        I am
white when it comes
        to my money.

It wasn't convulse
or moon-foolery —
I heard
white & money
& I saw Money, Mississippi—
Skintight Levi's on a flat ass
need more than lust—
In my head
rain really
lopes,
really
rains.

Identified by Fingerprint

Unseasonably exposed to fuchsia,
I left that Southern town

knotted to why-what
secrecy.   *#Like my*

first time on a ferris wheel.
Complex (n.) Psychonalysis:

"emotionally significant ideas completely
 or partly repressed that cause psychic

con-
flict   leading to"

Gentler and older men, throughout my
twenties & thirties, whose lives were living rooms

of emotions and mirrors. *Arboreta*; they refused
to be branches on which sediment could roost.

Brand-New Sheets

Elbowing people & pauses
I say, *bouge!* "Move Over!"
plenty of lime & seltzer
brie & bubbly in the fridge.
Fartin' & fallin'
on brand-new sheets
it's my house and I live here.
Christmas strokes the she in me
what it is to love somebody
to spoon & be spooned
that's life, riding high in April
in the bathroom, in the car, in the study
their aunt my auntee
mom is "ma"
To love somebody
this sunlight around the house—
Our queer bicycles under the stoop.

What can I do with this feeling?

Some people don't schwa the A in her name,
they won't *ah* it, like they do for ago & anonymous.
Into secondhand enunciation, they dote on & long-
chew the alphabet's first letter, its crunch-gristle, A-dele.

The Manhattan in me says Adele.   Toodle loo—
I, too, sing along, with & through, her numbered albums,
the years & poundage of a nightingale's wake turbulence:
Right under my feet is air made of bricks.

But when I close my eyes, throw back my head,
sway it from side-to-side in a bop that might
daze the confused who think they know
what *no* in its haze & flesh looks like,
I am spinning in belief, foaming
for the next *yes* note—before,
between & after a swallow of spit,
waiting for the spoils of Aretha, Gladys, & Leela,
to be took to the water.

& for some reason,
I get stuck somewhere,
on the edge of something,
listening to Joss & Amy & Dusty.

Coloratura—
peony-splattered drama
atop bedside books.
Dear Adele,
25 strands me someplace
unlit & parched.

"Vulnerability, mistrust and melancholy,"
said *The New York Times* of Ta-Nahesi Coates'
We Were Eight Years in Power: An American Tragedy.
Sax the truth   let the poem say Amen,
politics edit & fickle my taste.

Sheep Headed to a Bad Market

> *Sorry, Miss Jackson*
> —Outkast

Defeat is personal. Limber hallelujahs
Lift heavy burdens.   Eyes
Fit for purple & further trough
                Gaze unravel—
Sheep headed to a bad market.
Hillary, hurt sister,   Where
Haven't we been?   Amid unwelcome
Wind, slow grind & two-step,
Let us slide electric & salsa
Drop-it & wobble while we wail.

Oaken in the Midst: Bleak Update to Mr. Baldwin

Between sleet & hydrangeas
oaken in the midst.
James Arthur Baldwin—
woolen & cashmere
clarity & contradiction.

Ascot for attic work,
lotion upon the ashen,
   Jimmy—
his hoot & language,
our maestro, mood, & message.

   Bleak update—
Systolic: America's Bleeding Noon—
He swung & hit again.
His cash is middle-named John & hood:
May 1, 1989: *New York Daily News*
$85,000 full-page headline

"BRING BACK THE DEATH PENALTY.
BRING BACK OUR POLICE!"
(Concerning The Central Park Five
   Exonerated in 2014):
Maybe hate is what we need

if we're gonna get something done.
To know well the beginning. . . .

The scurrying & collisions—
This White House is dyspeptic.
A Youngstown woman oh no's!:
He talks off the cuff like us. I'm tired of
suave and polished. I want my country back!

Exposed in a previous gale,
Texas legalized "same-sex" love:
Rachel and Nadine
Nesta and DaShawn.   Still,

The unleavened sides of poet & poem
thin my stride & pen,
like PrEP-era barebacking
or another ominous trend.

Aphorism

A bull
will need
his tail
to fan flies
out of his ass
for more than
one summer

"Think": *after Curtis Mayfield*
In the key of Beyonce's "Resentment"

The hours of the day are sleek, shelter under which I rebottle my
turpentine.
When last I saw you the rain surpassed whoop. The boring birthday party
Not yours or mine, was undeserving of 40,000 air miles; massive room
Scant warmth, no booze—what a weird-ass family.

With other lives to listen to, your company has come to dim my vigor.
Especially when we don't talk. I was mentioning a trip to Marrakesh
& visiting Koutoubia Mosque, made of red clay, & you continued
Playing *Angry Birds*. We have to do something about this.

With luck on our side, we may never need La-Z-Boy's or live-ins.
Remember Odell & Station, your two aces, their final fevers
& how lend-me-yesterday mauled their heads? Mom, you boil words
Down your way & to the roux with black pepper & bouillon:

"My health is my business, a twig between patient & doctor." A twig?
What is that supposed to mean? Unwired for whimsy & woe
I'd like to stash the winter between us in a yellow-striped box.
Be it magenta, beige, or lilac, I'm out of color for every crotchety.

Go ahead, wear black flats with floor-length skirts & trousers—
You, do you! With thyroid trouble, low iron & iodine & aversion
To anything uncanned—Ms. Fannie suggests oil of oregano & garlic.
Like family, rocks will be rocks; we flaunt our arrogance & shield.

Two rattler sightings this week?
Ask Ricardo or Uncle Al to mow the lawn.
I am off to Samba class.
Madrid is seven hours ahead of Montgomery.

The Music That Learns Us

Facing the blackboard,
the teacher whistles
a melody of marbled tenderness.
Entanglement,
intrigue or spook?
Perhaps,
in retrospect,
Monday thoughts
of cared-for cashmere
or the end bite
of Sunday's sweet potato.
It simmers & simmers,
the music that learns us;
The Mamas & the Papas
Queen Latifah singing
"California Dreamin'."
The ear is nobody's fool.

At Le Diplomate

for my sister Ruby Denise

1601 14th St. NW

Washington, DC 20009

Front window banquette—

Patient & citrus

How we sister & brother.

Obits

Tucked away

Tonight   We won't crossword

Repasts & funerals.

Instead we menu pinot soup

Holler   mignon   & mousse.

Are unabashed

Unpricked balloons

Hootenannying

Birthdays & fortunate brain surgery.

Our mother—

shawl frayed & idiomatic

—Live & let live—

Taught us how to scan the iris for bullshit.

Which man's neck-thick is worthy of lather.
Taught us that good beef is love.

Notes

Epigraph: Bobby "Blue" Bland: "Kiss Me To The Music" *Midnight Run* (1989).

Norphenia's Lament: I borrow a line from "Try a Little Tenderness," a song cemented and popularized by Otis Redding.

Note from Norphenia: *Everything's Out in the Open*: The italicized portion of the title is from a Johnnie Taylor song on *In Control* (1988).

Fastened to Roots, Love & Story: Mother Recalls a Ten-Pound Storm: I rearrange the lyrics from the song "I Say a Little Prayer," written by Burt Bacharach and Hal David.

After Ben Webster's 1959 Rendition of "Time After Time": The tune in the title and the line used in the poem are from the jazz standard. This particular cover is recorded on the album *Ben Webster and Associates*. I also borrow lyrics from "Tryin' to Love Two," recorded by William Bell on *Coming Back for More* (1977).

Epigraph: "Express Yourself" B-side "Living on Borrowed Time." *Express Yourself* (1970).

Hot Metal Cools Slowly into Law: Line and lyrics from two songs, "Muddy Water (A Mississippi Moan)": Bessie Smith's version and "Angel of the Morning." Whose version? Nina Simone's!

Elegy for Sabena: Two lines are from "Being Me," written and recorded by Abbey Lincoln. Ms. Lincoln's 1995 album *A Turtle's Dream* was near.

***Bird Alone*:** Written and recorded by Abbey Lincoln featuring saxophonist Stan Getz, *You Gotta Pay the Band* (1991); lyrics utilized via epigraph and throughout the poem.

2 June 2001: Before *What Happened, Miss Simone?* The italicized portion of the title is taken from a November 1970 *Redbook* quote/question by the late Dr. Maya Angelou and aptly used for the 2015 documentary, directed by Liz Garbus, chronicling the life of singer and pianist Dr. Nina Simone (1933-2003).

mid-poem sequence: lyrics from Bobby Womack's song/monologue "(They Long to Be) Close to You," *Communication* (1971).

Epigraph: I was introduced to "This Way Willoughby" through a friend born in 1943 in East Harlem, New York. According to her, the "Willoughby" was also a dance that kids shimmied down her East 101st Street block. In her youth, "all day long" was replaced by "all night long."

Kamasi, Muscadet, & Mary Lou Williams: "Leroy & Lanisha" is from Kamasi Washington's *Epic* (2015); though not mentioned, let me mention *Zoning* (1974) by Mary Lou Williams.

Identified by Fingerprint: Lyric from the song "First Time on a Ferris Wheel." Nancy Wilson's version bit its way through *Love, Nancy* (1994).

Oxford English Dictionary re: Complex (n.) Psychoanalysis.

Brand-New Sheets: Two italicized lines of note: Written by Nickolas Ashford and Valerie Simpson, Diana Ross's "It's My House" *The Boss* (1979).

"That's Life," popularized by Frank Sinatra; the mood of this poem relied on Aretha Franklin's cover from *Aretha Arrives* (1967).

What can I do with this feeling? That's still the question Curtis & Aretha, Mr. Mayfield & Ms. Franklin, writer & singer respectively, from "Hooked On Your Love" *Sparkle* (1976).

There's a line borrowed from Adele's "Melt My Heart to Stone," written by Eg White and Adele *19* (2008).

Sheep Headed to a Bad Market: Epigraph from Outkast's "Ms. Jackson" from *Stankonia* (2000).

"Think": *after Curtis Mayfield:* —In the key of Beyoncé's "Resentment:"

"Think (instrumental)" *Super Fly* (1972); "Resentment" *B' Day* (2006).

Acknowledgments

Grateful acknowledgment is expressed to the following journals, in which these poems first appeared, some under different titles and in earlier versions:

BOMB Magazine, Center for Book Arts Broadsides Reading Series, Clean Sheets, The Cortland Review, Four Way Review, Indolent Books HIV Here and Now, Margie Review, Red River Review, Southern Humanities Review, and *What Rough Beast*.

For years, I embodied this book in fragments; something fully clothed has landed. This incomplete list wishes to remember some of my seasonal and resident angels by name: my mother Ruby Edwards Leonard, beloved Carlos San Juan García and Antonia García Reyes, my sisters Diane Leonard, Marva Joyce Leonard, Vera Lee and Ruby Taylor; for laughter, counsel, and friendship Dr. Patricia Meade Leonard; friends and family: Dr. Obie Nichols, Chevelle Cromwell, Sandra Dee Anderson, Sonya K. Holley-Thompson, Jai Holley-Thompson, Roderick and LaTonya Riley, Shirley Alexander, Lise Esdaile, Ronald Ottaviano, Luca Ottaviano, Patrice Harris Kuss, Jintz Bagwell, Steve Mitchell, Rev. Stacie Weldon, Diego San Juan García, Yolanda San Juan García, Lucia San Juan García, Shirley Key Wells, Jerome Wells, Chuck Beckett, Nyia Eady, Pat Warrington, A.J. Muhammad, Bret Leonard,

Benjamin Leonard, Nina Leonard, Seth Norris, Imani Norris,
Brandon Leonard, Carson Phillips, Rev. Lewis Benson,
Hannah Risinger, Tracey A. Jackson, Iris Morales,
José Angel Figueroa, Trapeta Mayson, Paula Milo-Moultrie,
Edward Moultrie, Tonya Wilder, Joanne Artates,
Corinne Lestch, Dr. Bridget McCurtis, Georgette Thompson,
Barbara Barkoutsis, Marcus Marshall, Don Nakamura,
Lindsay Redding, Charmaine Page, Milton Porter,
Robert Hanselman, Otis Ramsey-Zöe, Vanessa Roberts,
Dr. LeRonn Brooks, Linda Susan Jackson, Yolanda Reynolds, and
Robert "Rocky" Schwarz.

I pour gratitude to poet and professor Alan Gilbert for immense
advisement and encouragement. And thank you to these
exceptional teachers: Gloria Johnson Ware,
JoEtta Maxwell, Novella B. Jones, Dorothy Parks,
Lyndon Wayne Austin, A. Van Jordan, Mark Bibbins,
Richard Howard, Elizabeth Alexander, the late
Reetika Vazirani, Wilka Neighbors and Dr. Maya Angelou,
Alan Felsenthal, Gerard Vezusso, Dr. Darryl DeMarzio,
Georgia C. Johns, and Dr. David Hansen.

In memoriam: Kimberly LaVerne Goggans,
Thelma Higgins-Pritchett, John Walter and
Mary Emma Edwards, (Big Moma and Big Daddy),
Annie Pearl Alexander, McKinley Butts, Kaleshia Leonard, Shakari
Taylor, Gladys Bell, my father Clarence Jackson, Jr., Carlos B.

Strong, Annie Paul Robinson, Aunt Catherine Riley and Mrs. Fannie Clark, whose home in Cape Coast, Ghana served as temple, Black library, bar and discotheque.

Thank you to Martha Rhodes for believing in this book. Boundless thanks to my editor and proofreader Bridget Bell. Added thanks to Carla Carlson, Ryan Murphy, Sally Ball, Clarissa Long and all the support at Four Way Books.

Lastly, I dedicate this effort to my nieces and nephews: Derell, Dasha, LeMarsha, Rakeshia, Jarvarus, Alfred, Kerick, Yandé, and Tori. Love to my maternal aunts, the Edwards sisters.

Rodney Terich Leonard was born in Nixburg, Alabama. An Air Force veteran who served during the Gulf War, his society profiles and poems have appeared in *Southern Humanities Review, Red River Review, The Huffington Post, BOMB Magazine, The Cortland Review, Indolent Books-What Rough Beast, Four Way Review, The New York Times, The Amsterdam News, The Village Voice, For Colored Boys* . . . (anthology edited by Keith Boykin) and other publications. He holds degrees from The New School, NYU Tisch School of the Arts, and Teachers College Columbia University. A *Callaloo* poetry fellow, he received an MFA in Poetry from Columbia University and currently lives in Manhattan.

Publication of this book was made possible by grants and donations. We are also grateful to those individuals who participated in our 2020 Build a Book Program. They are:

Anonymous (14), Robert Abrams, Nancy Allen, Maggie Anderson, Sally Ball, Matt Bell, Laurel Blossom, Adam Bohannon, Lee Briccetti, Therese Broderick, Jane Martha Brox, Christopher Bursk, Liam Callanan, Anthony Cappo, Carla & Steven Carlson, Paul & Brandy Carlson, Renee Carlson, Cyrus Cassells, Robin Rosen Chang, Jaye Chen, Edward W. Clark, Andrea Cohen, Ellen Cosgrove, Peter Coyote, Janet S. Crossen, Kim & David Daniels, Brian Komei Dempster, Matthew DeNichilo, Carl Dennis, Patrick Donnelly, Charles Douthat, Morgan Driscoll, Lynn Emanuel, Monica Ferrell, Elliot Figman, Laura Fjeld, Michael Foran, Jennifer Franklin, Sarah Freligh, Helen Fremont & Donna Thagard, Reginald Gibbons, Jean & Jay Glassman, Ginny Gordon, Lauri Grossman, Naomi Guttman & Jonathan Mead, Mark Halliday, Beth Harrison, Jeffrey Harrison, Page Hill Starzinger, Deming Holleran, Joan Houlihan, Thomas & Autumn Howard, Elizabeth Jackson, Christopher Johanson, Voki Kalfayan, Maeve Kinkead, David Lee, Jen Levitt, Howard Levy, Owen Lewis, Jennifer Litt, Sara London & Dean Albarelli, David Long, James Longenbach, Excelsior Love, Ralph & Mary Ann Lowen, Jacquelyn Malone, Donna Masini, Catherine McArthur, Nathan McClain, Richard McCormick, Victoria McCoy, Ellen McCulloch-Lovell, Judith McGrath, Debbie & Steve Modzelewski, Rajiv Mohabir, James T.F. Moore, Beth Morris, John Murillo & Nicole Sealey, Michael & Nancy Murphy, Maria Nazos, Kimberly Nunes, Bill O'Brien, Susan Okie & Walter Weiss, Rebecca Okrent, Sam Perkins, Megan Pinto, Kyle Potvin, Glen Pourciau, Kevin Prufer, Barbara Ras, Victoria Redel, Martha Rhodes, Paula Rhodes, Paula Ristuccia, George & Nancy Rosenfeld, M. L. Samios, Peter & Jill Schireson, Rob Schlegel, Roni & Richard Schotter, Jane Scovell,

Andrew Seligsohn & Martina Anderson, James & Nancy Shalek,
Soraya Shalforoosh, Peggy Shinner, Dara-Lyn Shrager,
Joan Silber, Emily Sinclair, James Snyder & Krista Fragos,
Alice St. Claire-Long, Megan Staffel, Bonnie Stetson, Yerra Sugarman,
Dorothy Tapper Goldman, Marjorie & Lew Tesser, Earl Teteak,
Parker & Phyllis Towle, Pauline Uchmanowicz, Rosalynde Vas Dias,
Connie Voisine, Valerie Wallace, Doris Warriner, Ellen Doré Watson,
Martha Webster & Robert Fuentes, Calvin Wei, Bill Wenthe,
Allison Benis White, Michelle Whittaker, and Ira Zapin.